Real-Life Reads

The Life of a
MEDIEVAL
KNIGHT

by Ruth Owen

Series consultant:

Suzy Gazlay, MA
Recipient, Presidential Award for Excellence in Science Teaching

Ruby Tuesday Books

Published in 2015 by Ruby Tuesday Books Ltd.

Copyright © 2015 Ruby Tuesday Books Ltd.

Editor: Mark J. Sachner
Designer: Emma Randall
Production: John Lingham

Photo Credits:
Alamy: 10, 16, 28–29; Bridgeman Images (Royal Armouries, Leeds, UK): 11 (bottom); Bridgeman Images (Saint Louis Art Museum, Missouri, USA): 9 (right); Getty Images: 13 (right), 15, 17; Public Domain: 7, 13 (bottom), 19, 23 (top), 26; Shutterstock: Cover (Raulin), 4–5 (Raulin), 6 (Jorisvo), 8–9, 11 (top), 12, 20–21 (Boykov), 22–23, 24–25 (PLRANG), 27 (Raulin), 31.

Library of Congress Control Number: 2013920126

ISBN 978-1-909673-54-0

Printed and published in the United States of America

For further information including rights and permissions requests, please contact our Customer Service Department at 877-337-8577.

Contents

Into Battle

Imagine the horrors of a bloody battlefield. Hundreds of soldiers are fighting.

Swords clash against swords. Deadly maces and battle-axes smash into armor. Horses snort and kick at the soldiers. Dying men are trampled beneath the horses' hooves. This was the world of the **Medieval** knight.

Knights were highly trained fighting men. They rode into battle on powerful warhorses. The horrors of the battlefield did not frighten these brave warriors.

5

The World of the Knight

Knights lived in England, France, and other countries in Europe. They fought in wars during the Medieval period.

The Medieval period was a very violent time. Powerful leaders, such as kings and princes, often invaded other countries. They went to war to win land and power.

This photo shows part of an embroidered artwork called the Bayeux Tapestry. The tapestry is nearly 1,000 years old. The picture shows the Battle of Hastings in 1066. The battle was between knights from England and France.

A knight fought for a king, prince, or lord. In return, he was given rewards such as farmland or a castle. There were warrior knights in Europe for around 500 years, from AD 1000 until the 1500s.

Over the centuries, knights became an important group of people. They weren't just soldiers. They were also wealthy members of the upper class, or **aristocracy**.

This painting shows the Battle of Nájera in 1367. English and French armies fought this battle in Spain. The painting shows knights on horseback and large numbers of foot soldiers.

On the battlefield, a knight fought against other knights. He also fought against ordinary foot soldiers. He was trained to use many different weapons.

At the start of a battle, a knight charged at the enemy on horseback. He carried a long, spear-like weapon called a **lance**. He used the lance to knock enemy knights from their horses. He also used it to stab enemy soldiers.

A lance was about 14 feet (4.3 m) long. It was made of wood with a sharp metal point.

Sword

Shield

Knights also fought with swords, battle-axes, and maces. A knight could attack his opponents with these weapons from his horse. He also used them when fighting on foot. To protect his body, a knight might carry a wooden shield.

A battle-ax was like a can opener for armor. It could crush and pierce through metal.

A mace was a club-like weapon. It could smash into armor and crush the person's body inside.

9

A Knight's Armor

Knights wore armor to protect their bodies during battles. Over the centuries, they wore many different designs of armor.

The earliest knights wore tunics, leggings, and gloves made of metal chainmail. They also wore chainmail hoods called coifs. The tops of their heads were protected by metal helmets. Some helmets had a nosepiece. These helmets were called nasal helmets.

Nasal helmet

Coif

Chainmail tunic

In the 1300s, knights began to wear much larger helmets. These helmets covered their whole heads. The great helm helmet had thin slits for seeing through. It also had tiny holes to let air into the helmet.

Chainmail was made of small metal rings linked together.

This great helm helmet is from the late 1300s.

Eye slits

Air holes for breathing

Suits of Armor

Sometimes, knights wore long, sleeveless coats over their chainmail. These coats were called surcoats.

Once knights began to wear helmets that covered their faces, they couldn't be recognized. So each knight had his own picture symbol called a coat of arms. The coat of arms was shown on a knight's surcoat and shield.

A coat of arms

A surcoat

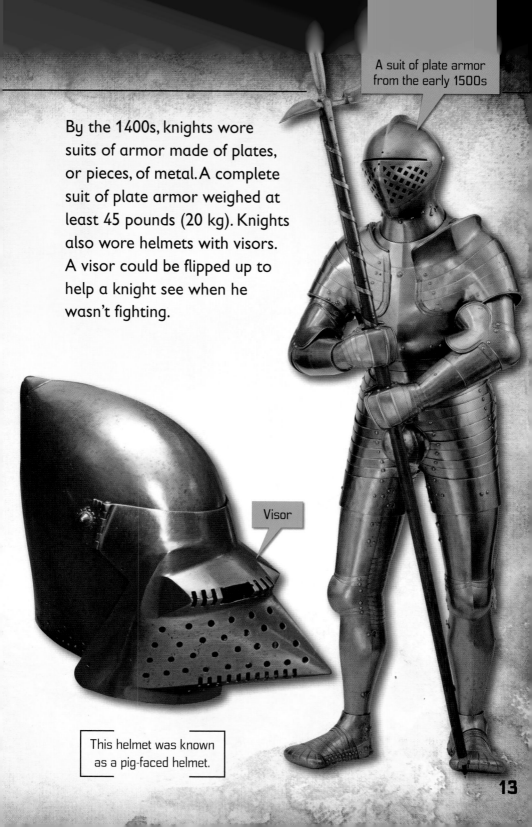

By the 1400s, knights wore suits of armor made of plates, or pieces, of metal. A complete suit of plate armor weighed at least 45 pounds (20 kg). Knights also wore helmets with visors. A visor could be flipped up to help a knight see when he wasn't fighting.

Visor

This helmet was known as a pig-faced helmet.

A knight rode into battle on a fast, strong stallion. This horse was known as a warhorse or *destrier*.

A warhorse was trained by riding it past servants who were shouting, banging drums, and waving banners. This stopped the horse from being afraid on a noisy battlefield. Warhorses were also trained to kick their knights' opponents!

A knight and his horse fought as a team. A good warhorse followed orders instantly. He might have to run, stop, twist, and turn. He had to carry the knight to just the right position to attack an opponent.

In battle, the enemy might try to kill a knight's horse. So warhorses wore armor called barding.

A knight in armor and a warhorse wearing metal barding

Pages and Squires

Only boys from rich families could afford to become knights. To buy armor, weapons, and several warhorses would cost about $300,000 in modern money!

A knight began his training as a child. He became a page, or servant, to a knight. He served the knight's meals and cleaned his clothes. At about 15, a page became a **squire**. Now, the trainee knight cleaned his knight's armor and weapons. He also cared for the knight's horses.

Trainee knights learned to ride and use a lance. They practiced by hitting a wooden target called a *quintain*. They also learned to sword fight using wooden swords.

This reconstruction shows a squire practicing using a lance against a quintain.

Becoming a Knight

When a knight went off to war, his squire went, too. A faithful squire helped his knight put on his armor. He helped prepare the knight's weapons and warhorse for battle.

A squire also practiced his fighting skills with his knight. If a squire was brave and skillful, he became a knight in his early twenties.

A squire was made a knight in a dubbing ceremony. He knelt before an important person, such as a king, queen, or lord. That person then tapped the squire on the shoulder with a sword.

Once a young man became a knight, he lived by a set of special rules. These rules were called the **chivalric code**.

The Chivalric Code

Here are some of the rules that a knight lived by on the battlefield and in everyday life.

- Be brave and fight fairly
- Be loyal to the king, prince, or lord whom you serve
- Love God and the church
- Always defend a lady
- Always protect the poor and helpless

This painting shows a squire being dubbed, or knighted, by a royal lady such as a queen.

19

The Joust

Knights took part in competitions called jousts. These competitions helped knights practice their riding and fighting skills.

During a joust, two knights rode at each other at high speed. Each knight carried a wooden lance.

Modern-day riders take part in a reconstruction of a Medieval joust.

A knight was not allowed to hit his opponent's body or horse with his lance. He had to hit his opponent's shield. Sometimes, a knight's lance shattered when it hit the shield. This earned the knight points. A knight also won points if he knocked his opponent off his horse.

Cheering crowds watched jousting competitions. Just like modern sports stars, knights who were good at jousting became famous.

The Hunt

A knight usually owned a castle or large manor house. He might also own lots of land, including farmland and forests.

A knight would go hunting on his land. He hunted for food and to practice his riding and killing skills. Hunters on horseback might chase a deer with hunting dogs. They chased the animal until it was exhausted. Then a knight would kill the deer with a sword or spear.

Knights also went hunting with falcons. These birds were trained to catch animals such as rabbits, ducks, and pheasants. The birds caught their prey and then carried it back to their owners.

Bodiam Castle in England was built by a knight in the late 1300s.

This painting is from a Medieval book about hunting.
The book was produced in the 1300s.

A falcon

Many Medieval knights went on expeditions known as the **Crusades**.

In the Medieval period, many parts of the world were home to mostly Christians. Others were home to mostly Muslims. The city of Jerusalem was very important to both religions. In about 1087, Muslims and Christians began competing for Jerusalem and other holy places.

Christian church leaders asked knights from Europe to go on a Crusade to win Jerusalem from the Muslims. For several hundred years, Christian knights went on several Crusades. They fought to try to win land and power for the church. Many fighters on both sides were killed. It was a terrible and violent time.

This reconstruction shows knights riding into battle.

During a battle, a knight used all his fighting skills.

When charging the enemy, he had to aim his lance. He had to protect his own body with his shield. He also had to ride hands-free at top speed. It took huge skill and strength to spear an enemy with a lance.

Once on the ground, a knight fought with his sword. Sometimes, a knight held the sword's hilt, or handle, with his right hand. He then held the blade with his left hand. This was called half-sword fighting.

This Medieval illustration shows a knight half-sword fighting against an enemy.

Half-sword fighting allowed a knight to make powerful, thrusting movements. He could push his sword through a gap in his opponent's armor. He might even thrust his sword through the eye slits of his enemy's helmet!

On the battlefield, a knight followed the chivalric code. This meant he could show **mercy** to a fellow knight during a fight.

Sometimes, a knight captured an opponent and kept him prisoner. After the battle, the losing knight had to pay a **ransom** to be released.

This bronze statue shows a knight named Edward, the Black Prince. The statue is on top of the prince's tomb. The tomb is in Canterbury Cathedral in England.

At other times, however, knights were killed. After a battle, men called **heralds** searched the battlefield. They looked for the bodies of dead knights. The bodies were then sent back to the knights' homes to be buried.

The tombs of many knights are inside cathedrals and other historic buildings. Sometimes, the tombs are decorated with a statue of the knight. These Medieval warriors lived hundreds of years ago, but they are still remembered today.

Glossary

aristocracy (air-iss-TAHK-ruh-see)
A group of important, often wealthy, people in society. Aristocrats, such as lords and knights, were more important than farmers and other working-class people. They were not as important as the royal family, though.

chivalric code (SHI-vuhl-rik KODE)
A set of rules that Medieval knights lived by. The code affected every part of a knight's life, from fighting in battles to how he treated poorer people who lived around him.

Crusade (kroo-SAYD)
A military expedition carried out by Medieval Christian knights, usually to fight for lands also claimed by Muslims.

herald (HAIR-uhld)
A person who carried out official duties for a lord or king, such as delivering messages to other important people. Heralds also helped organize battles and kept records of who was killed.

lance (LANSS)
A long, wooden, spear-like weapon used by a Medieval knight on horseback.

Medieval (med-ee-EE-vuhl)
From the time in history known as the Medieval period, or Middle Ages. This period lasted for about 1,000 years, from around AD 400 to about 1500.

mercy (MUR-see)
Showing kindness or forgiveness, especially to an enemy.

ransom (RAN-suhm)
A payment made to a captor so that he or she will release a prisoner.

squire (SKWIRE) A trainee knight and servant to an older knight. Being a squire was not a lowly job. It was an honor to serve a knight.

Index

Read More

Dargie, Richard. *Knights and Castles (The Age of Castles)*. New York: Rosen Publishing (2008).

Murrell, Deborah. *Knight (QEB Warriors)*. Mankato, MN: Black Rabbit Books (2009).

Learn More Online

To learn more about Medieval knights, go to
www.rubytuesdaybooks.com/knight